GEOMETRY IS EVERYWHERE!

VISTA®
HIGHER LEARNING

Boston, Massachusetts

T0026517

MATH

Right angles? Triangles?
Lines, areas, and formulas?
Do we really need geometry?
You learn about it for math
class. It's just for tests, right?
No way!

Look around! Geometry is
everywhere. People use it
at home. They use it at work.
You can use it, too!

You want to change your bedroom. How much paint do you need? Use geometry! Use a formula. Find the **height**. Find the **length**. Multiply. That is the area. Then, **calculate** the paint you need.

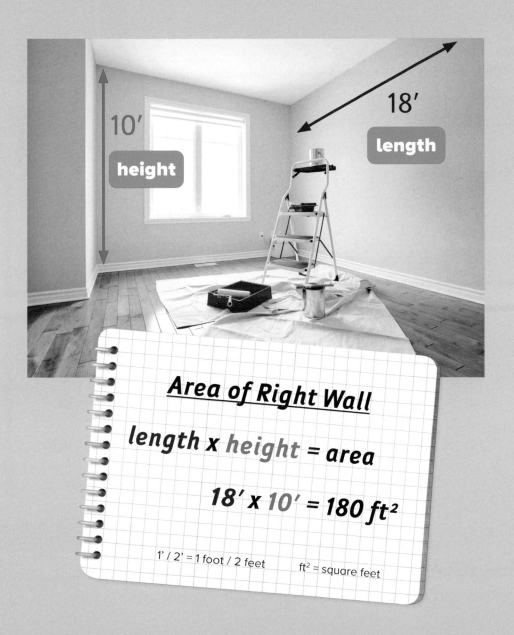

10′

height

18′

length

Area of Right Wall

length **x** height = area

18′ x 10′ = 180 ft²

1′ / 2′ = 1 foot / 2 feet   ft² = square feet

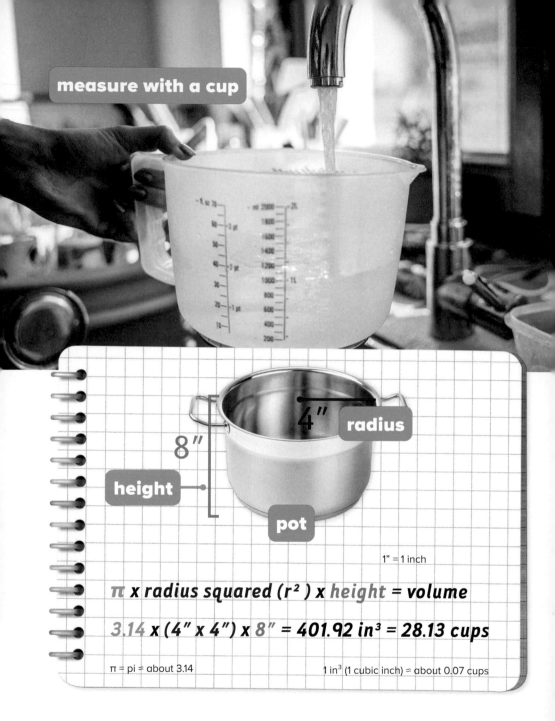

measure with a cup

8"

height

4" radius

pot

1" = 1 inch

$$\pi \text{ x radius squared } (r^2) \text{ x height } = \text{volume}$$

$$3.14 \text{ x } (4" \text{ x } 4") \text{ x } 8" = 401.92 \text{ in}^3 = 28.13 \text{ cups}$$

π = pi = about 3.14   1 in³ (1 cubic inch) = about 0.07 cups

You're in the kitchen. You want to make soup.
Which pot do you use? Do you **measure** with
a cup? No! Use a formula. Find the volume.

You want to make a garden. How big will it be? Use a formula. Make a plan.

Do you want a border, too? How much wood do you need? Measure the sides. Find the length. Find the **width**. Multiply by two.

perimeter

border

garden

My Garden Plan

100'

20'

10'

100'

length x width = area

20' x 10' = 200 ft²

(2 x length) + (2 x width) = perimeter

(2 x 20') + (2 x 10') = 60'

Time for art class. Do we need geometry? Yes! Pictures have many **shapes**. Do you want a picture to look real? Use angles. Measure them. Draw shadows. There! Now your picture looks **3-D**!

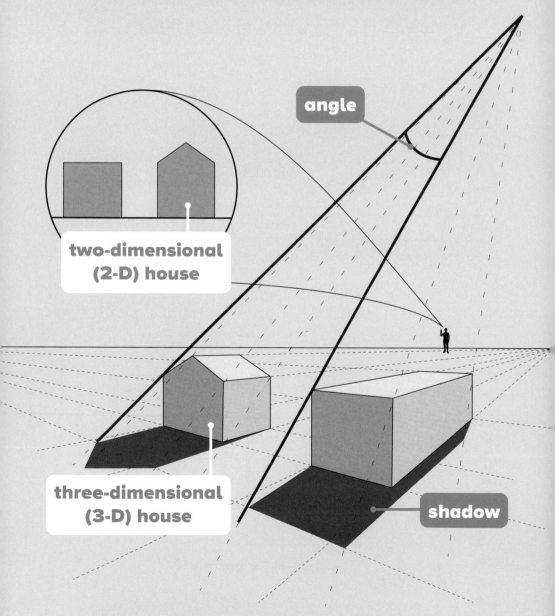

angle

two-dimensional (2-D) house

three-dimensional (3-D) house

shadow

All artists use geometry. They use shapes to make **patterns**.

pattern

They use shapes in interesting ways.

Some art looks more real. But there is geometry here, too! Look at the lines. Look at the shapes. Look at the angles and shadows.

artist

There is geometry
in our clothes, too.
Fabrics have patterns.

fabric

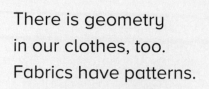

People use geometry to
make clothes. They cut
shapes. They sew angles.

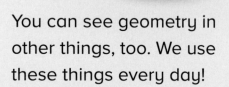

You can see geometry in
other things, too. We use
these things every day!

People use geometry with video. They use it in movies. It shapes the pictures. It makes things look 3-D. People use geometry to make video games. Some games are all about shapes!

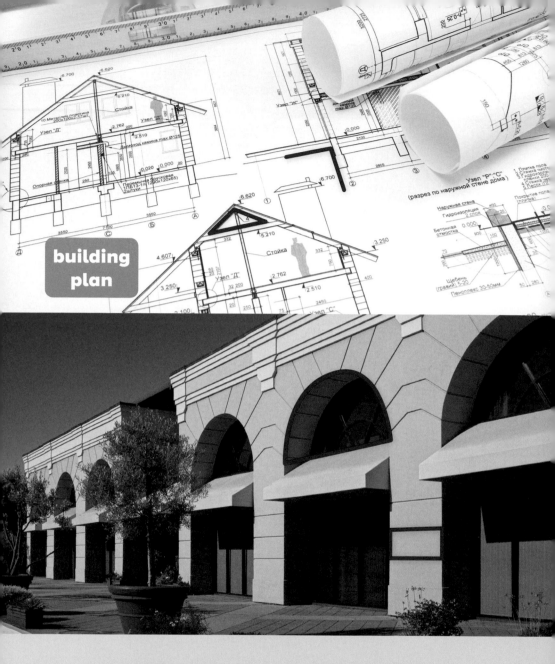

building
plan

Geometry is very important in buildings. People use it in plans. They use it to build houses and schools. They use it to build hospitals and stations.

Buildings won't stay up without the right geometry. What makes our houses safe? Geometry!

People also use geometry to build other things.
They measure angles. They make shapes.
They use triangles, squares, and circles.

Long ago, people
used geometry.

People need it today, too. Do you want
to build something? You need geometry!

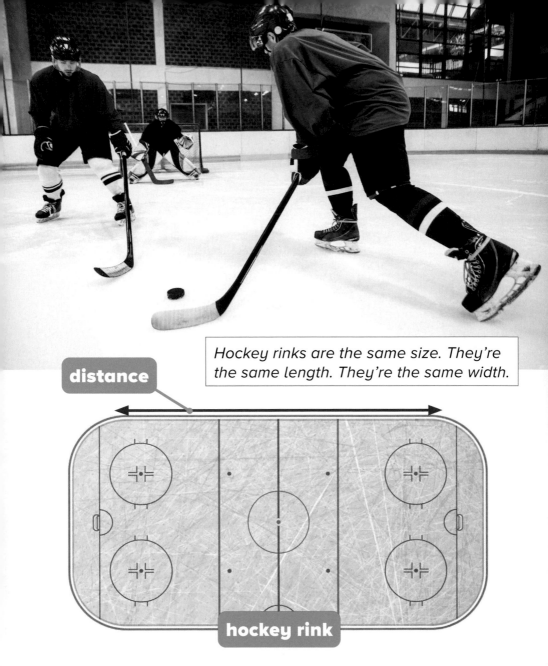

Hockey rinks are the same size. They're the same length. They're the same width.

distance

hockey rink

Geometry is even important in sports! Look at the hockey rink. See the shapes? See the lines? They're always in the same place. They're always the same **distance** apart. Hockey rinks are the same size. It makes the game fair.

Look at the hockey stick. See the angle? The players can hold it well. It stays on the ice. Players can hit the puck better.

Look at the puck. It's a shape, too. It's a circle. Wait, no! It's not. It's a cylinder!

Players use geometry. They look at angles. They look at shapes. Players think fast!

Do you like nature? It's full of geometry!
Animals use it to make things. There are shapes
in plants and trees. There are shapes in the sky.

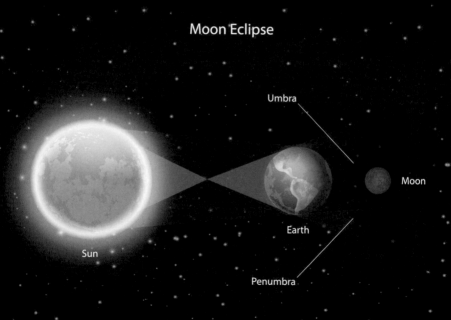

Moon Eclipse

Umbra

Moon

Earth

Sun

Penumbra

People use geometry to learn about space. It
helps measure things. It helps calculate size
and distance.

So, you see? Geometry isn't just for math class. It's not only for tests. It's all around us. Take time to learn about it. Make geometry a part of your life. Geometry is everywhere!

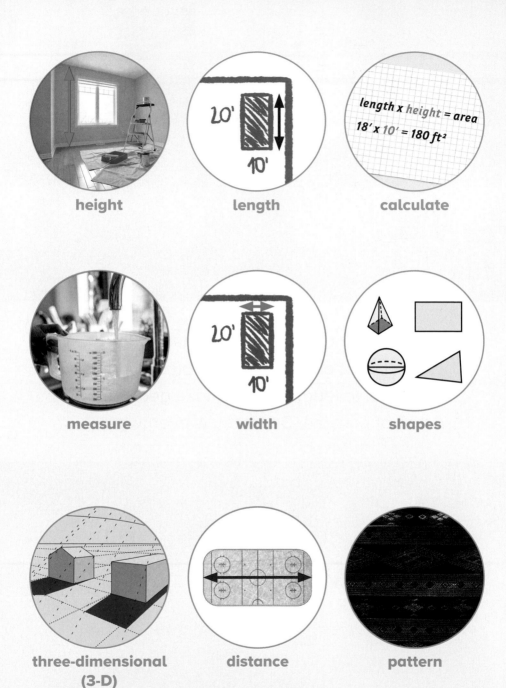

height

length

length x *height* = area
18' x 10' = 180 ft²

calculate

measure

width

shapes

three-dimensional (3-D)

distance

pattern